BEARS AT THE BEACH

BEARS AT THE BEACH

COUNTING 10 TO 20

BY NIKI YEKTAI

THE MILLBROOK PRESS
BROOKFIELD, CONNECTICUT

For my brother Elian N. Kulukindis,
who is very good at counting.

With thanks to Barbara Lucas for the idea...

N.Y.

Library of Congress Cataloging-in-Publication Data
Yektai, Niki.
Bears at the beach : counting from 10 to 20 / by Niki Yektai.
Summary: Presents the numbers from ten to twenty using illustrations
of the activities of three bear families at the beach.
ISBN 0-7613-0047-3 (lib. bdg.) ISBN 0-7613-0022-8 (trade)
1. Counting—Juvenile literature. [1. Counting.] I. Title.
QA113.Y45   1996
513.2'11—dc20   95-41583   CIP   AC

A Lucas-Evans Book
Published by The Millbrook Press
2 Old New Milford Road
Brookfield, Connecticut 06804

10 umbrellas

11 bears

12 bags

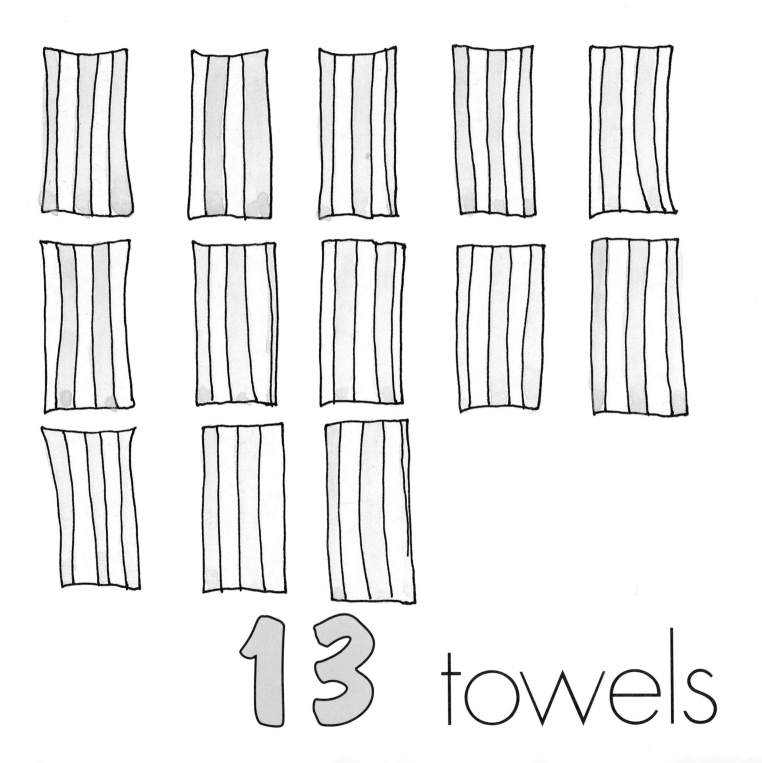

13 towels

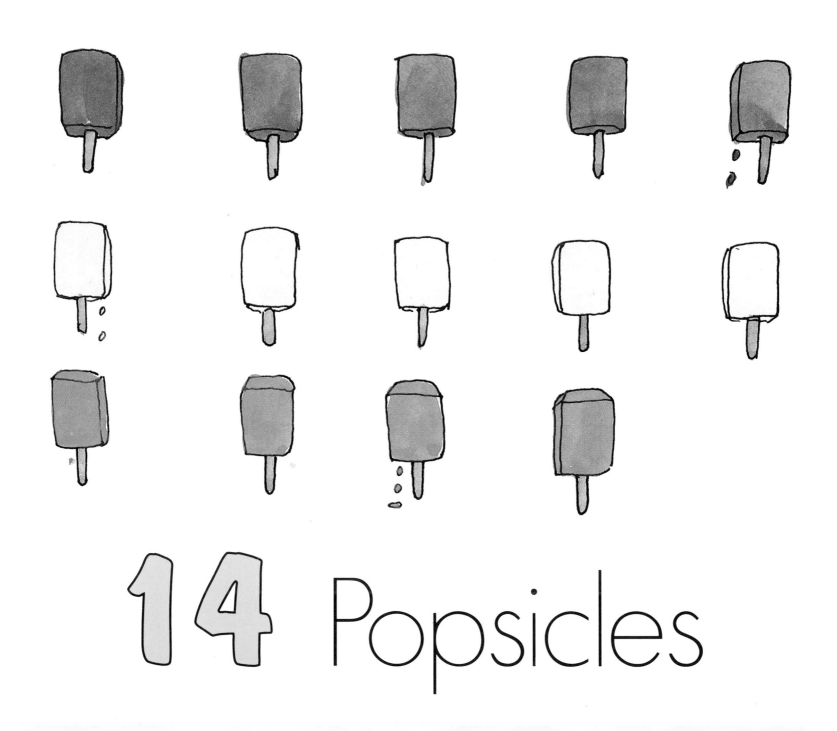

14 Popsicles

15 sandwiches

16 shells

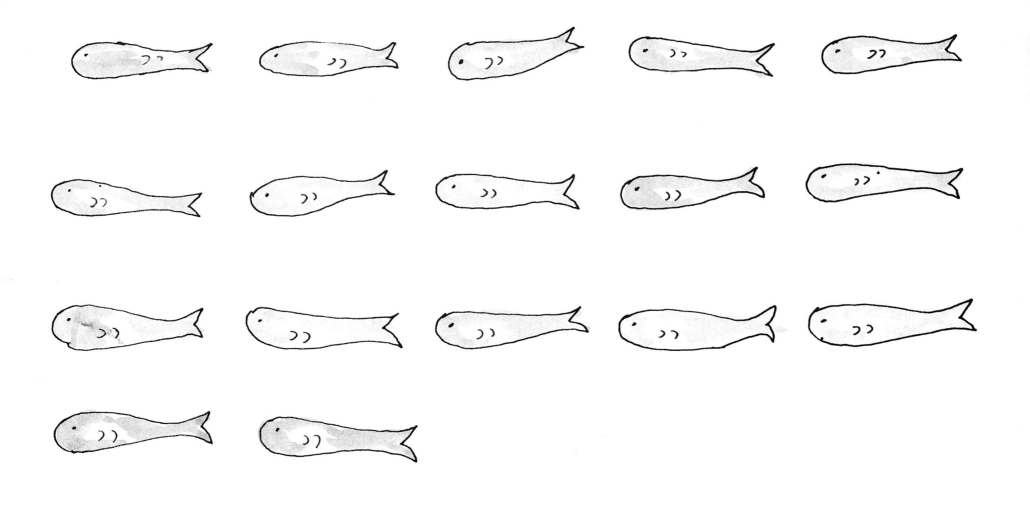

17 fish

18 pails

19 stones

castles

ABOUT THE AUTHOR/ILLUSTRATOR

This is the 7th picture book that Niki Yektai has written. Her earlier publications include *What's Missing* and *What's Silly* and *Bears in Pairs*. She is also the author of a novel for older children entitled *The Secret Room*. *Bears at the Beach* is the author's debut as a book illustrator. The illustrations for the book are the original watercolor sketches that she prepared merely as a guideline for what she thought would be an illustrator assigned to the book.

Ms. Yektai has a Masters Degree in education from New York University and she teaches remedial reading in New York City. She has studied art in many places, most notably watercolor classes with Nancy Howell and David Dewey. She perpetually studies writing with Margaret Gabel at the New School in New York.

When Mindy Saved
Hanukkah

story by
ERIC A. KIMMEL

pictures by
BARBARA McCLINTOCK

SCHOLASTIC INC.
New York Toronto London Auckland Sydney
Mexico City New Delhi Hong Kong Buenos Aires

ISBN-13: 978-0-545-13887-1
ISBN-10: 0-545-13887-6

12 11 10 9 8 7 6 5 4 3 2 1   8 9 10 11 12 13/0

Printed in the U.S.A.   40

This edition first printing, September 2008

Special thanks to the Eldridge Street Synagogue,
the Lower East Side Tenement Museum,
Rabbi Melinda Panken,
and Zehava Berger for reviewing the book.

The text type was set in 13-point Scotch Roman.
Hand lettering by Paul Colin · Book design by David Saylor
Barbara McClintock's art was rendered in watercolor, black ink, and gouache.

To Dianne

— E.K.

To Mom and Helmut, with love

— B.M.

Once upon a time, a little family named Klein lived behind the walls of the Eldridge Street Synagogue.

It was the day before Hanukkah, and everyone was getting ready. Mama was busy cooking. Mindy was teaching her little brother Hillel to play dreidel.

Tick-tock! Tick-tock! The clock on the wall ticked loudly. Two o'clock. Papa was still not home.

"Where can he be?" Mama asked. "Getting one Hanukkah candle can't take so long."

Suddenly a commotion came from the doorway.

"Help!" a voice cried out. Mindy and Hillel ran to see who it was.

It was Papa. He didn't have a candle. Instead, he had sprained his ankle.

"What happened?" Zayde asked. "You look like you went through a potato grater."

"Well," Papa gasped. "I guess someone finally did something about those mice in the synagogue!"

"And what was that?" asked Mama.

"They got a cat. A fierce Antiochus of a cat! Like that king who tried to wipe out the Jewish people in the days of the Maccabees. If I hadn't seen him out of the corner of my eye just before he pounced, I wouldn't be talking to you now!"

"Cats? What cats?" Zayde sniffed. "Back in the Old Country, when I was a boy, *we* had cats..."

"Cats are cats, wherever they are," Bubbe interrupted. "They eat rats. They eat mice. And they'll eat us Kleins if they get the chance. So now we have a problem. What are we going to do about the Hanukkah candle?"

"Without a candle, it just won't seem like Hanukkah," Mama said.

"I want Hanukkah!" Hillel began to cry.

"Don't cry, Hillel. I'll go," said Zayde. "Cats don't scare me. Why, when I was boy..."

"But you're not a boy now," said Bubbe. "You're not going anywhere."

"If I don't go, who will?" Zayde asked.

No one answered.

"What about me?" said Mindy.

"What about you?" everyone exclaimed at once.

"I can climb better and run faster than anyone."

"It's too dangerous," said Bubbe.

"How can you carry a candle home by yourself?" Mama asked.

"I can roll it," Mindy answered.

"It could work," Papa said. "Otherwise we won't have one."

"We *have* to have a candle!" Hillel wailed.

"That settles it," said Mindy, "I'm going."

Mama, Papa, Bubbe, and Zayde looked worried.

Hillel grinned.

Mindy was sure she could do it.

Everyone helped Mindy get ready.

Hillel gave her his lucky stone.

Bubbe hung a bag of garlic around her neck.

"Ptu! Ptu! Ptu!" Mama spat three times.
She pinched Mindy's cheeks and threw salt
over her shoulder for good luck. *"Keynahora!"*
she said. "No evil eye!"

"Superstitions — feh!" Zayde scoffed.
"Just keep your eyes open and you'll be fine."
Papa gave Mindy his best climbing hook,
and together they saw her off to the doorway.

"Be careful, Mindy," everyone warned as they kissed her good-bye.

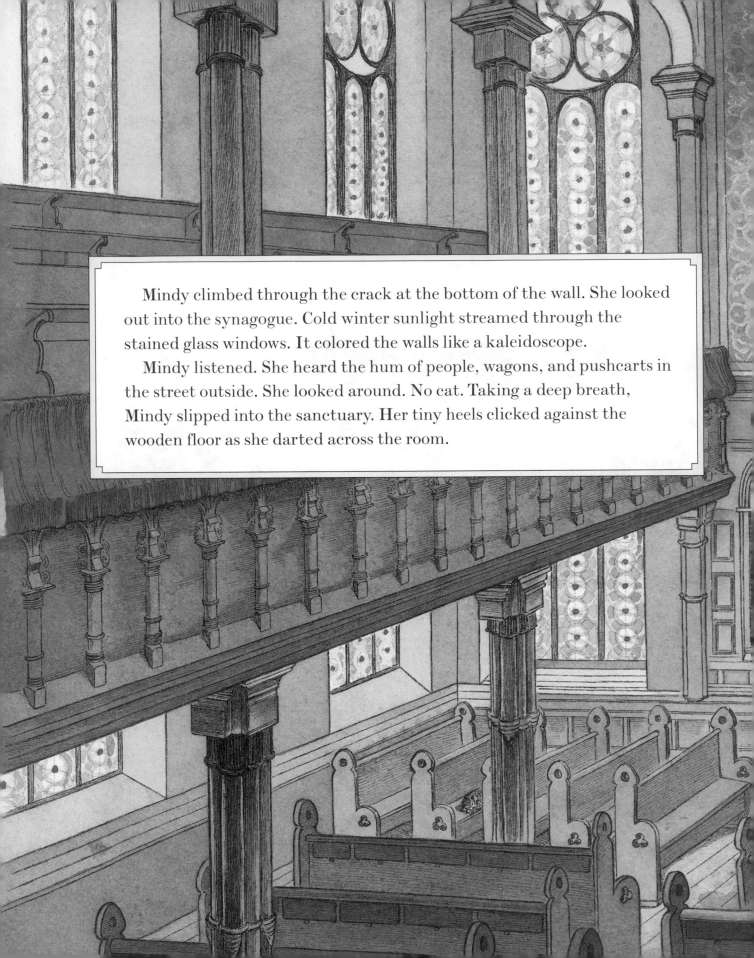

Mindy climbed through the crack at the bottom of the wall. She looked out into the synagogue. Cold winter sunlight streamed through the stained glass windows. It colored the walls like a kaleidoscope.

Mindy listened. She heard the hum of people, wagons, and pushcarts in the street outside. She looked around. No cat. Taking a deep breath, Mindy slipped into the sanctuary. Her tiny heels clicked against the wooden floor as she darted across the room.

Mindy was out of breath by the time she reached the four steps that led to the ark. Papa had spoken of a stray candle that had rolled to the back of a high shelf there last year. Mindy swung the climbing hook around her head. She threw it up to the first step. The hook bit into the carpet. Mindy pulled herself up, hand over hand. When she reached the next step, she listened. All was quiet.

Mindy threw the hook again and climbed up the next step. Two more times. Finally she reached the top of the steps. Her heart pounded.

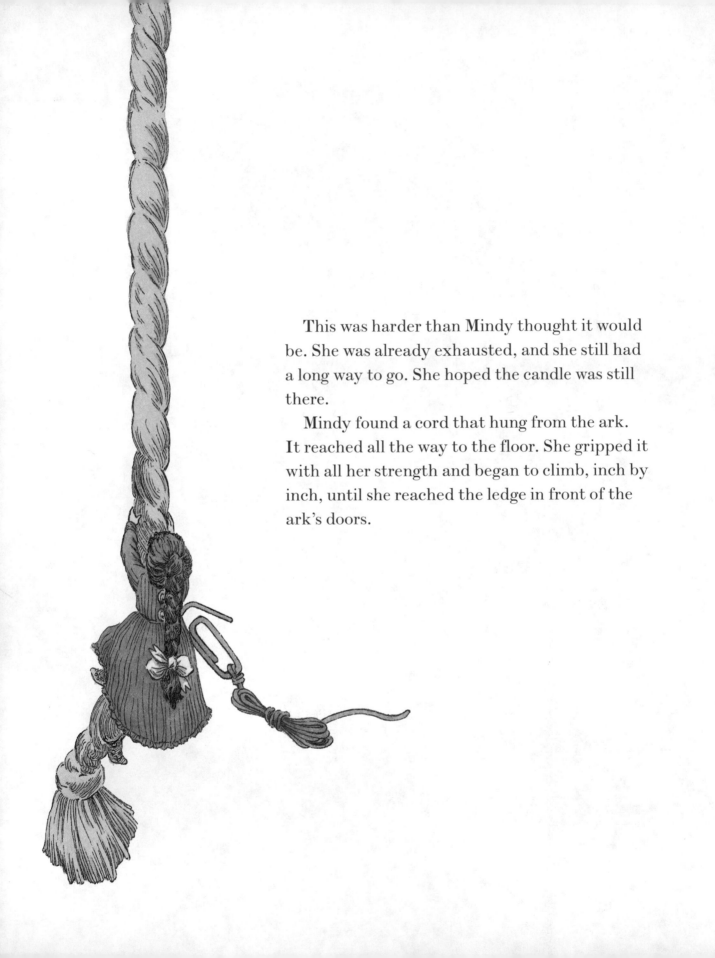

This was harder than Mindy thought it would be. She was already exhausted, and she still had a long way to go. She hoped the candle was still there.

Mindy found a cord that hung from the ark. It reached all the way to the floor. She gripped it with all her strength and began to climb, inch by inch, until she reached the ledge in front of the ark's doors.

Mindy pulled the door with all her might.
It opened a crack, and she slipped inside.

The Torah scrolls loomed over her head. A *yad* pointed its huge silver finger down at her.

High above, she could see the shelf she was looking for. But how could she get there?

A *lulav*, the palm branch left over from Sukkot, leaned against the wall. Seeing it gave Mindy an idea. She began to climb the *lulav* as if it were a tree.

When she reached the shelf, Mindy squeezed behind a prayer book and peeked around a brass menorah. She tiptoed past a brand new box of Hanukkah candles.

Then she saw it at the back of the shelf. The extra candle! Mindy felt like shouting, but she didn't dare make any noise.

Mindy rolled the candle across the shelf and pushed it over the edge. It grazed the Torah as it fell to the ground. Mindy hurried after it. She climbed down the *lulav*, slipped out of the ark door, then started to slide down the cord — when suddenly. . .

GRRRWW!

A shadow pounced. The cord whipped around as Mindy held tight. The cat leaped. His claws reached for Mindy. She felt them tear at the hem of her dress.

The cat crouched in front of the ark. He stared at Mindy with bright yellow eyes.

I'm trapped, Mindy thought. *He's going to eat me for sure!*

But before the cat could pounce, a familiar voice rang out.

"Antiochus, you fiend! You leave Mindy alone!"

It was Zayde. Mindy hardly recognized him. With his beard and fierce eyes, Zayde looked just like a Maccabee of old. Tied to his left arm was a bottlecap shield. The thimble on his head made a shining helmet. He held a toothpick in his right hand like a spear. Stuck on the end was a large piece of pickled herring that had fallen under the radiator after last Saturday's bar mitzvah.

"Don't worry, Mindele. You climb down and get the candle. Leave this pussycat to me."

Zayde turned to the cat. "Come, Antiochus! A Maccabee has arrived to drive you from the temple again!"

But just as the cat was about to charge at Zayde, Zayde flung the toothpick like a javelin. The piece of pickled herring went sailing across the room. The cat flew after it. "What cat can resist a piece of herring?" Zayde laughed.

Mindy jumped down from the cord to the floor. She pushed the candle down the steps and rolled it across the room as fast as she could. When she reached the crack in the wall, Mama, Papa, and Bubbe leaped out to help her. Together they pulled the candle inside, just as Zayde came running. "Wait for me!" he yelled.

They pulled him inside, too. And not a moment too soon. The cat had devoured the pickled herring and was still hungry. Sharp claws scratched at the wall. Big yellow eyes gleamed through the crack. But the Kleins were all safely inside. And they had their candle!

One big candle makes lots of little candles. And the Kleins made plenty. Mama and Bubbe made latkes, and applesauce, and jelly doughnuts for a feast that lasted all eight nights of Hanukkah. The Pequeños from Shearith Israel came. They brought a big basket of presents for everyone. The Littles came downtown from Temple Emanu-El along with their friends, the Katans, who were visiting from Jerusalem. Everyone had a wonderful time. They all agreed it was the best Hanukkah ever.

On the eighth night, Papa asked Mindy and Zayde to light the menorah. "Without their courage, we wouldn't have had candles for Hanukkah," he said.

"Mindy's a hero," Hillel added. "She wasn't afraid of Antiochus the cat. And she brought back a candle — just for me!"

"Zayde's a hero, too," Mindy said. "He saved me from Antiochus with a piece of pickled herring. He's as brave as any Maccabee."

"As the Maccabees of old proved to King Antiochus," Zayde said proudly, "you don't have to be big to be mighty."

"Heroes come in all sizes," Mama agreed. "Some are big. Some are little. Some lived long ago. Some live today."

And some even live behind the walls of the Eldridge Street Synagogue.

Glossary

Antiochus (an-tee-O-kus): Antiochus Epiphanes was a Greek king who ruled over what is now Syria, Lebanon, and Israel from 175-163 B.C.E. His attempt to force the people of Judea to worship pagan gods sparked the Maccabean Revolt.

Ark: The cabinet where Torah scrolls are kept.

Bubbe (BUH-bah): Yiddish for "Grandma."

Dreidel (DRAY-del): A four-sided top, with a letter on each side, used to play a Hanukkah game. The letters are: Nun (נ); Gimel (ג); Hay (ה); and Shin (ש). They stand for the Hebrew words, *Nes Gadol Haya Sham* — "A Great Miracle Happened There."

Eldridge Street Synagogue: This is a real place! It is located at 12 Eldridge Street on Manhattan's Lower East Side. Built in 1887, this exquisitely beautiful house of worship was a great source of pride to Jewish immigrants from Eastern Europe.

Hanukkah (HA-nu-kah): Hanukkah, the Festival of Lights, celebrates the rededication of the Temple in Jerusalem in 165 B.C.E. The Hebrew word *Hanukkah* means "dedication."

Herring (HER-ing): A kind of fish, usually served salted or pickled.

Keynahora (kahn-ah-HAH-rah): A dialect form of the Yiddish *Keyn Eynhore*, a superstitious phrase said to ward off the evil eye.

Klein (KLINE): "Little" in Yiddish or German. The characters' names "Pequeño" (Spanish) and "Katan" (Hebrew) also mean little!

Latke (LAHT-kah): A potato pancake.

Lulav (LOO-lav): A palm branch, held together with sprigs of myrtle and willow, which is used during Sukkot, the Feast of Tabernacles. Some Jewish people save their *lulavs* until Passover. The dried palm branches are then used to kindle the ovens that bake matzot, the unleavened bread used during Passover.

Maccabee (MACK-a-bee): A name given to Judah the Hasmonean, a guerrilla leader who recaptured Jerusalem from the Greeks and founded an independent Jewish state in 165 B.C.E. No one is certain what "Maccabee" means. The most widely accepted definition is "Hammerer."

Menorah (men-O-rah): A candleholder with eight branches, plus an extra socket for the *shamash* or "helper" candle. The *shamash* is used to light the other candles. The eight lights recall the miracle that happened during the rededication of the Temple, when a single day's supply of oil burned for eight days. The menorah is kindled each night during the eight nights of Hanukkah.

Torah (TOE-rah): A handwritten parchment scroll containing the Hebrew text of the first five books of the Bible. These are Genesis, Exodus, Leviticus, Numbers, and Deuteronomy. This text is also known as the Pentateuch, or the Five Books of Moses.

Yad (YAHD): A silver rod with a pointing hand at the end, used by the Torah reader to find and keep the right place during the Torah reading. The Hebrew word means "hand."

Zayde (ZAY-dah): Yiddish for "Grandpa."